MEGAFAST CARS

Thanks to the creative team:
Senior Editor: Alice Peebles
Designer: Lauren Woods and collaborate agency

Original edition copyright 2015 by Hungry Tomato Ltd.

Hungry Tomato™
A division of Lerner Publishing Group, Inc.
241 First Avenue North
Minneapolis, MN 55401 USA

For reading levels and more information, look up this title at www.lernerbooks.com.

Main body text set in Economica Bold.
Typeface provided by Tipotype.

Library of Congress Cataloging-in-Publication Data

The Cataloging-in-Publication Data for *Megafast Cars* is on file at the Library of Congress.

ISBN 978-1-4677-9363-6 (lib. bdg.)
ISBN 978-1-4677-9581-4 (pbk.)
ISBN 978-1-4677-9582-1 (EB pdf)

Manufactured in the United States of America
1 – VP – 12/31/15

MEGAFAST CARS

by John Farndon
Illustrated by Mat Edwards and Jeremy Pyke

HUNGRY
TOMATO™

CONTENTS

MEGAFAST CARS

In this book, we feature a selection of the world's fastest cars. And they are fast—really, really fast. It's not just their frighteningly high top speeds, but also their astonishing acceleration. When a Lamborghini Aventador takes off at full throttle, the air crackles with a mighty roar and the driver is flung back in the seat with breathtaking force as the car gains speed in seconds.

In the time it takes you to read this sentence, it will be over a quarter of a mile away!

And now it's half a mile away...

SENSATIONAL SCHUMACHER

Some say the greatest racing driver of all time was the Argentinian Juan Fangio, who raced in the 1950s when Grand Prix racing was brutally dangerous. Others say it was the Brazilian Ayrton Senna, who won 41 races before being tragically killed at the Imola racetrack in 1994, at the age of just 34. But many think it is the German Michael Schumacher, who scored 91 wins between 1991 and 2012.

ROAD SPEEDS

On motorways in the UK and many highways in the USA, cars are allowed to travel at no more than 70 mph. For most people that's quite fast enough! But all the cars featured in this book can go way faster than that. That means they can only reach their top speeds on private roads and racetracks. If a Hennessey Venom could keep up its top speed of 270 mph all the way, it could drive from New York to Los Angeles in less than ten hours!

THAT WAS HOW FAST?!

It is easy to see when a plane or a motorcycle, a car or a truck is megafast. But *how* do you know just how fast it is? Speed is the distance that something moves in a certain time. It is the distance covered divided by the time. If a jet plane travels 2,000 miles in two hours, it travels 1,000 miles in each hour. So we say its speed is 1,000 miles per hour, or mph. The top speeds for the machines in this book are given in mph.

SPEED MATTERS

Speeds for vehicles on the ground are typically given in mph (miles per hour) or km/h (kilometers per hour). Rockets may shoot away from Earth at over 11 km per second. If a plane flies faster than sound, its speed may be compared to the speed of sound in similar conditions. This speed is called a Mach number. So a plane flying at the speed of sound (typically over 700 mph) is said to be flying at Mach 1.

GETTING QUICKER

One way of seeing how fast something moves is to measure how quickly it gains speed—that is, its acceleration. You can actually measure how much something accelerates every second. But with fast vehicles, the acceleration is usually given by how long it takes to reach a particular speed, typically from a standing start, 0 mph. The shorter the time, the faster the acceleration. So acceleration figures for a superbike that takes just 2.9 seconds to get from a standstill to 60 mph would be 0–60 in 2.9 seconds. That's megafast!

AGAINST THE CLOCK

The most accurate way of measuring top speed is to measure how long a vehicle takes to cover an exact distance, such as a mile. That's how the official top speeds in this book were measured. To ensure split-second accuracy, the clock is triggered to start and stop when the vehicle cuts through a beam of light.

SPEED DIAL

Speed against the clock is average speed. Police speed guns and speedometers in cars, trucks, and motorcycles register the speed at any one instant. Speed guns fire a radar beam and detect the way it bounces off a moving vehicle. With speedometers, an electronic sensor counts the number of times small magnets on the wheel sweep past it each second and converts that into a speed in mph to display on the dashboard or LCD screen inside the car.

BUGATTI'S GRAND MASTER

The Bugatti Veyron is fast—very, very fast! In fact, it's the fastest production car in the world. When its monster-power engine roars to life it generates 987 brake horsepower, or bhp. That's about 12 times as powerful as an average family car. With that kind of muscle, it can reach nearly 270 mph. That's so fast it needs special aerodynamic shaping to stop it from taking off!

BURN-UP

At 250 mph, the Veyron's tires will last only 15 minutes. Its 26.4-gallon fuel tank goes dry in 12 minutes. It also consumes 12,000 gallons of air per minute—as much air as one person breathes in four days.

Top Speed	50	100	200

THE FIRST SUPERCAR

Back in 1939, Bugatti made the first supercar—the supersleek 57SC Atlantic. *SC* stood for "supercharger," which increases the supply of compressed air to an engine. This meant the 57SC could reach 120 mph. Only four were built, and three survive to this day. It still looks pretty amazing, with its beautiful streamlined body.

POWER
987 bhp

0-200 MPH
20.2 seconds

TOP SPEED
269 mph

ENGINE
8 liter,
16 cylinder

TORQUE
1,992 lb-ft
max

PRICE
$1,960,000
plus tax!

300   400   500   **269 mph**

VIKING THUNDER

A thousand years ago, the Viking warriors of Sweden were awed by Thor, god of thunder. Now awesome thunder bursts out of Sweden in the roar of the Koenigsegg Agera R, one of the world's fastest production cars. *Agera* means "take action"—and the Agera can accelerate from 0-62 mph in just 2.8 seconds and may be able to reach 273 mph.

STOP!!!!

With such fast cars, good brakes are vital, and the Agera's brakes are phenomenal. It holds the world record for blasting from a standstill to 200 mph, then screeching to a halt again—all in just 24.96 seconds.

Top Speed | 50 | 100 | 200

POWER
1,100 bhp

0-200 MPH
17.68
seconds

TOP SPEED
273 mph

ENGINE
5 liter V8 twin
turbocharged

TORQUE
811 lb-ft

PRICE
$1,650,000
plus tax!

GHOST RIDER

The Agera's interior
has eerie "ghost light"
controls. LED lights
seem to appear out of
nowhere on solid aluminium buttons. The light
shines through almost invisible micro-holes.
Newsflash: The Koenigsegg One:1 will be the
world's most powerful road car, with an engine
generating 1,322 bhp—and it's eco-friendly,
running on biofuel.

300   400   500   273mph

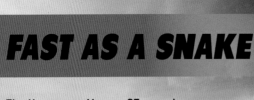

FAST AS A SNAKE

The Hennessey Venom GT was always megafast. But its follow-up, the F5 Venom, is even faster! Twin turbochargers give the V8 engine a scary 1,400 bhp of power, and the carbon-fiber body is incredibly light: just 2,866 lb. The F5 may soon blow the Bugatti Veyron away with speeds up to 290 mph.

THE FURY OF A TORNADO

The F5 is named after a tornado. Not just any tornado, but the most powerful tornado of all on the Fujita scale! Winds rip around an F5 tornado at 261 to 318 mph. So the F5 Venom and a tornado are an awesomely perfect match!

VEYRON VS. VENOM

On one particular whirlwind run at the Kennedy Space Center in 2014, the Venom GT roared up to 270.49 mph. That made it faster than the record-breaking Veyron's 269.86 mph. But the Venom only made the run one way, not two ways. This meant that the Veyron held on to its crown as the world's fastest production car…just.

Top Speed | 50 | 100 | 200

POWER
1,400 bhp

0-200 MPH
14.51 seconds

TOP SPEED
290 mph

ENGINE
7 liter V8

TORQUE
1,155 lb-ft

PRICE
$1,200,000 plus tax!

300   400   500   290mph

STRIPPED FOR SPEED

When racing car designer Gordon Murray built the McLaren F1 in 1991, he wanted it to be the fastest road car ever. He stripped the car down to essentials to keep it light, and added a super-powerful BMW V12 engine. The F1 outgunned all other cars of the time with a top speed of 240 mph, a record not beaten for nearly a decade.

Top Speed	50	100	200

MIDDLE OF THE ROAD?

Most supercars have just two seats. But the F1 has three. The driver sits in front in the middle, with the passengers either side and slightly behind. This position gives the driver unusually good visibility.

POWER
627 bhp

0-200 MPH
28 seconds

TOP SPEED
240 mph

ENGINE
6.1 liter V12

TORQUE
480 lb-ft

PRICE
$840,000

The bird on McLaren's badge is a kiwi, a symbol of New Zealand, birthplace of company founder Bruce McLaren.

RACE WINNER

Most of the cars entering the famous Le Mans 24-hour race are specially built racing cars. But in 1995, McLaren entered a team of modified F1s and came in first, third, fourth, and fifth! The secret was the F1's reliability.

300   400   500   **2240 mph**

THE ULTIMATE IN SPEED

Few cars can match the Bugatti Veyron when it comes to
top speed. But the SSC Ultimate Aero is one. It may be the
fastest American car ever, and it overtook Bugatti to claim
the record of 256.14 mph for the world's fastest production
car in 2007. Bugatti took back the lead in 2010 with a run
of 269 mph, but the Ultimate remains among the leaders.

Top Speed	50	100	200

POWER
1,287 bhp

0-200 MPH
16 seconds

TOP SPEED
256.14 mph

ENGINE
6.9 liter V8

TORQUE
1,112 lb-ft

PRICE
$750,000

SUPERLIGHT BODY

The Ultimate Aero is not quite as light as air, but almost. Take off the doors, hood, and trunk lid, and its superlight carbon-fiber body shell weighs just 131 lb – that's lighter than most adults!

ROCKET TESTED

The Ultimate Aero's smooth body slips through the air with minimum air drag, thanks to tests in the wind tunnel at NASA's Langley Research Center– where they normally test space rockets!

300	400	500	2256.14 mph

FIGHTING FAST

Sharply creased and flat, the Lamborghini Aventador is unusually shaped for a car. But the shape is inspired by one of the ultimate aircraft: the Lockheed F-117 Nighthawk.

The F-117 is a stealth fighter plane that uses unusual flat surfaces to make it almost invisible to radar. It helps that the Aventador simply vanishes very quickly…

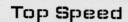

Top Speed	50	100	200

LAMBO DOORS

One of the special features of the Aventador is its Lamborghini trademark "scissor" doors, sometimes known as "Lambo doors." Unlike gullwing doors that swing out and up, scissor doors pivot straight upwards at the front, to open like a scissor blade.

RACING BULL

Lamborghini's badge features a charging bull, and many Lamborghinis are named after bulls that became famous in bullfighting, such as Miura, Diablo, and Reventón. Aventador is the name of a bull that won many bullfights in Saragossa in Spain in 1993.

POWER
690 bhp

0-60 MPH
2.9 seconds

TOP SPEED
230 mph

ENGINE
6.5 liter V12

TORQUE
508 lb-ft

PRICE
$400,000

300   400   500   **230 mph**

FORMULA FOR SPEED

Formula One cars are the fastest racing cars in the world. With ultralight bodies and incredibly powerful engines, they can hurtle around the race track at speeds of well over 200 mph. To keep the cars stable they are built very low. But there's not much room for the driver, who has to squeeze in and lie back less than an inch from the ground!

Top Speed	50	100	200

STAYING ON TRACK

Extremely wide tires help Formula One cars stick to the track like glue. So does their aerodynamic body shape, which pushes the car down like aircraft wings in reverse. This is called the ground effect. Formula One rules limit just how much cars can use the ground effect. But it means these cars can corner at incredible speeds.

FLAGGING IT UP

Race marshals signal to drivers with special flags. These also show up on the driver's computer display, since they're not always easy to see at high speeds. Each flag sends a particular message (see below).

Checkered flag: the race is over—you are the winner;
Red: race stopped; Yellow: danger—slow down;
Blue: you are about to be lapped; Black: return to pit;
Yellow and red stripes: slippery track; Green: all clear;
Black/orange circle: faulty car; Black/white: you are cheating; White: slow-moving vehicle on the track

POWER
750 bhp

0-100 MPH
4 seconds

TOP SPEED
233 mph

ENGINE
1.6 liter V6

TORQUE
260 lb-ft

PRICE
Tens of millions of dollars—materials alone cost $2,600,000!

300   400   500   **233 mph**

JET-PROPELLED

If you want to break the world land speed record, you need jet power. That's what the cars built to beat the record use. These jet-propelled blazers are the world's fastest cars. The record holder is Richard Noble's Thrust SSC, which reached 760.343 mph on October 15, 1997, driven by Andy Green. It was so fast it broke the sound barrier, traveling faster than sound!

GOING FOR THE RECORD

Thrust SSC (right) still holds the world land speed record. But at least half a dozen other cars are trying for it, including the North American Eagle (above left), Jet Black, Aussie Invader, and Bloodhound SSC (above center). They hope to reach 1,000 mph!

Top Speed	100	240	380

SPIRIT OF AMERICA

American Craig Breedlove (b. 1937) loves speed. After a successful career as a racing driver, he turned to the land speed record—and broke it five times in cars called Spirit of America. In 1964 Breedlove became the first person to drive at over 500 mph. In 1965 he became the first to reach 600 mph, and his wife, Lee Breedlove, drove at 308 mph, making them the fastest couple on Earth.

POWER
110,000 bhp

0-600 MPH
16 seconds

TOP SPEED
760.343 mph

ENGINE
Two Rolls-Royce turbofans

THRUST
50,000 lb

PRICE
Unknown

520   660   800   760.343 mph

THE WHEEL THING

Up until 1963, all land speed records were achieved in cars driven by their wheels, like ordinary road cars. Then Craig Breedlove broke the record in a jet-propelled car. Since then all record breakers have been jet-propelled. But there are still people who want to make wheel-driven cars travel at mega-high speeds.

Top Speed

50	100	200

POWER
2,500 bhp

0–431 MPH
77 seconds

TOP SPEED
462 mph

ENGINE
6 liter V8

TORQUE
1,313 lb-ft

PRICE
Unknown

RECORD BREAKERS

In this lineup are three amazing record breakers. In the foreground is Donald Campbell's Bluebird CN7, the last wheel-driven car to hold the land speed record, reaching 403.10 mph in 1964. Nudging through the middle is Buckeye Bullet, a battery-powered car, built by Ohio students, that reached 307.666 mph. Coming up fast in the background is George Poteet's Speed Demon.

WHIZZING WHEELS

In 2013, American George Poteet fired the Speed Demon up to well over 400 mph across Bonneville Salt Flats. His average speed of 439.562 mph over the measured mile was a world record for a piston-engined, wheel-driven car. On one run he reached 462 mph!

300   400   500   **462 mph**

FLAMING TAKEOFF

Top Fuel drag racing is all about blistering acceleration. Using nitromethane-fueled engines, cars are powered to incredible speeds of 330 mph from a standing start in the blink of an eye. They cover the measured 1,000 feet of track in just 3.7 seconds! Nitromethane, which is used to fuel rockets, burns slower than gasoline, so the exhausts shoot out flames of burning fuel, adding to the drama.

DON'T MOVE!

The most famous Top Fuel dragster is Tony Schumacher's US Army, painted in the colors of the US Army. It is the fastest-accelerating machine on land, accelerating five times as fast as gravity. Its 8,000-hp engine can rip it up to over 330 mph in just 1,000 feet.

FUNNY CARS

If you want to see ordinary cars transform into monstrously speedy dragsters, then look for Funny Car events. Funny cars have hugely tilted carbon-fiber bodies that look like ordinary cars. But they are mounted on specially built chassis and equipped with megapowerful engines. The most successful funny car driver is John Force, who now drives cars that look like Chevrolets.

Top Speed	50	100	200

POWER
8,000 bhp

0-330 MPH
3.736
seconds

TOP SPEED
330.23 mph

ENGINE
Bore and
stroke:
4.187 x 4.500

TORQUE
Unknown

PRICE
$10,199

| 300 | 400 | 500 | 330.23 mph |

WANT TO KNOW MORE?

Bugatti Veyron

This car uses special Michelin PAX tires that are twice as wide as the tires on a normal car. If one ever gets punctured, it can be run flat until you get to a garage to get it repaired. But if you ever need a new set, you have to order it from Michelin in France at a cost of well over $40,000.

Koenigsegg Agera

With the One:1 version of the famous Agera, Koenigsegg's aim was to create a track racing car that could also be used on the street. With one horsepower for every kilogram of weight, the One:1 had a blistering pace that could reach 273 mph. But only six were ever built. Two sold in Britain and four in China.

Lamborghini

When the German car tuners Mansory got their hands on a Lamborghini Aventador, they created the Carbonado. They replaced all the body panels with ultralight carbon fiber and added twin turbochargers to boost power to 1,600 hp. Not everyone likes the result, but it is superfast, with a top speed of 230 mph.

Bonneville Salt Flats

The most famous place in the world for land speed record attempts is Bonneville Salt Flats in Utah, USA. The Flats are a natural flatland formed by salty water evaporating to leave just a vast, smooth crust of salt. It was here that George Easton and John Cobb vied for the world land speed record in the 1930s, and Craig Breedlove claimed his world records in the 1960s in Spirit of America.

Formula One

The cars in Formula One are designed to tight regulations that are continually changing. In the 2015 season, for example, regulators were worried about race teams going too far in stripping off weight for extra speed. So they insisted that every car must weigh more than 1,548 lb (702 kg) without fuel. They also regulated against more extreme nose designs intended to improve stability.

High-Speed Dragster

The US Army Top Fuel dragster accelerates faster than any other car on the planet, covering 1,000 feet in just 3.736 seconds. That means the G-forces when it takes off from the start are huge. The driver feels a force of 5G—that is, five times the force of gravity. And when he throws out the parachutes to slow down, he experiences a force of 5G the other way. Tough ride!

INDEX

GLOSSARY

Aerodynamic Shaped so that air flows smoothly around

Acceleration How quickly something gets faster

Brake horsepower (bhp) The power direct from the engine; 1 horsepower can move 550 pounds one foot every second, written as 550 ft-lb per second

Carbon fiber Special tough, light material made by reinforcing plastic with fibers of carbon

Thrust The pushing force of a jet

Torque The force with which something turns, measured in pounds per feet (lb-ft)

Turbocharger A device to boost an engine's power by using the exhaust gases to turn a turbine that rams extra fuel and air into the cylinders

THE AUTHOR

John Farndon is Royal Literary Fellow at Anglia Ruskin University in Cambridge, UK. He has written a huge number of books for adults and children on science, technology, and nature, and has been shortlisted four times for the Royal Society's Young People's Book Prize.

THE ILLUSTRATORS

UK artist Mat Edwards has been drawing for as long as he can remember. He began his career with a four-year apprenticeship as a repro artist in the ceramic industry and has been a freelance illustrator since 1992.

Jeremy Pyke left the RAF to follow his passion for illustration. He has worked on many children's books and uses oil, watercolor, computer-generated illustration, and 3-D animation.

Picture Credits (abbreviations: t = top; b = bottom; c = center; l = left; r = right)

© www.shutterstock.com: 7 br, 8 tc, 8 br, 9 cr, 9 bl

7 tl , 7 tr David Acosta Allely/www.Shutterstock.com. 9 tr i4lcocl2/www.Shutterstock.com. 30 tl Max Earey/www.Shutterstock.com. 30 cr Zavatskiy Aleksandr/www.Shutterstock.com. 30 bl Fingerhut/www.Shutterstock.com. 31 tl John Blanton/www.Shutterstock.com. 31 cr cjmac/www.Shutterstock.com. 31 bl Action Sports Photography/www.Shutterstock.com